DINOSAURS

THE FASTEST
THE FIERCEST
THE MOST AMAZING

Written by Elizabeth MacLeod
Illustrated by Gordon Sauvé

Consultant: Dr. Philip J. Currie, Head, Dinosaur Research,
Royal Tyrrell Museum of Palaeontology

VIKING

MOST POPULAR

This dinosaur used to be known as *Brontosaurus*, but today scientists call it *Apatosaurus*. It's probably the most popular and famous dinosaur because its skeleton was one of the first really large ones found. *Apatosaurus* was a plant eater and was always on the move searching for food. It probably travelled in family groups, with the babies in the middle for protection. This dinosaur's body was longer than two school buses, and its tail was even longer. It may have used its tail as a whip to protect itself from enemies.

STRANGEST TAIL

When *Euoplocephalus* swung its powerful, club-shaped tail, other dinosaurs got out of the way. One swing and it could knock another dinosaur off its feet. *Euoplocephalus* was protected all over with thick bony plating — it even had bony eyelids. It needed all the protection it could get because it was very slow and awkward. This strong giant had a good sense of smell, but probably it also used its nose to make snorting calls to keep in touch with other *Euoplocephalus*.

STRANGEST NOSE

Scientists think *Edmontosaurus* had special flaps of skin on its snout. It could fill them with air to help make its roars loud and clear. That made it easier for *Edmontosaurus* to call and find its family or to warn of danger. Even though this dinosaur was a plant eater, it had more than 1000 teeth! Scientists digging up *Edmontosaurus* skeletons have found the pattern of its skin pressed into the rock around its bones, so we know it had skin like an elephant or a rhinoceros.

BIGGEST PTEROSAUR

Quetzalcoatlus wasn't a dinosaur. It is known as a pterosaur or "winged lizard" because it had wings and could fly. That's something no real dinosaur could do. But it lived around the same time and in the same places as dinosaurs. Like birds today, *Quetzalcoatlus* had hollow bones, and it's a good thing, because it was as big as a small airplane! It was probably a scavenger, like a vulture, and spent much of its time soaring high in the sky looking for its next meal.

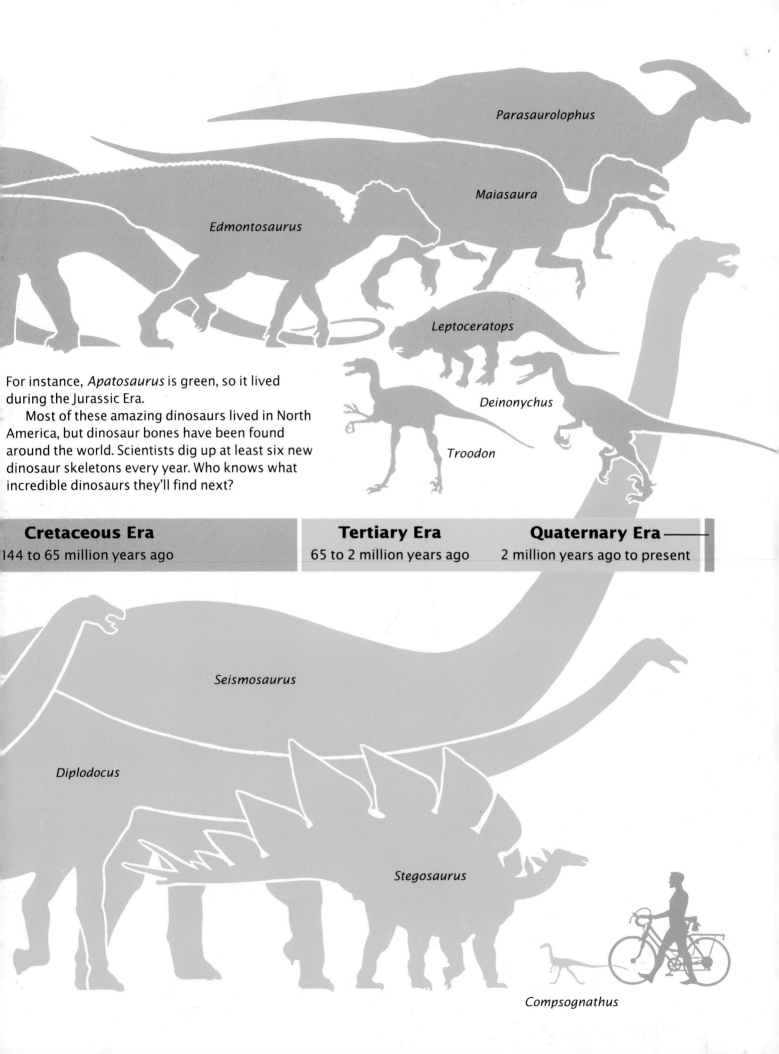

Parasaurolophus

Maiasaura

Edmontosaurus

Leptoceratops

For instance, *Apatosaurus* is green, so it lived during the Jurassic Era.

Most of these amazing dinosaurs lived in North America, but dinosaur bones have been found around the world. Scientists dig up at least six new dinosaur skeletons every year. Who knows what incredible dinosaurs they'll find next?

Deinonychus

Troodon

Cretaceous Era	**Tertiary Era**	**Quaternary Era**
144 to 65 million years ago	65 to 2 million years ago	2 million years ago to present

Seismosaurus

Diplodocus

Stegosaurus

Compsognathus

With much love to Mom and Dad – E.M.

*To my wife Barbara, and my son, Daniel,
for all their love and support – G.S.*

*Many thanks to Dr Philip J. Currie, Head of Dinosaur Research,
Royal Tyrrell Museum of Palaeontology. He gave generously
of his time to make valuable suggestions on both the text and
illustrations.*

VIKING
Published by the Penguin Group
Penguin Books USA Inc., 375 Hudson Street, New York, New York 10014, U.S.A.
Penguin Books Ltd, 27 Wrights Lane, London W8 5TZ, England
Penguin Books Australia Ltd, Ringwood, Victoria, Australia
Penguin Books Canada Ltd, 10 Alcorn Avenue, Toronto, Ontario, Canada M4V 3B2
Penguin Books (N.Z.) Ltd, 182–190 Wairau Road, Auckland 10, New Zealand

Penguin Books Ltd, Registered Offices: Harmondsworth, Middlesex, England

First published in Canada by Kids Can Press Ltd, 1994
First published in Great Britain by Viking Children's Books, 1995
First published in the United States of America by Viking,
a division of Penguin Books USA Inc., 1995

1   3   5   7   9   10   8   6   4   2

Text copyright © Elizabeth MacLeod, 1994
Illustrations copyright © Gordon Sauvé, 1994
All rights reserved

Library of Congress Catalog Card Number: 94-61733

ISBN 0-670-86026-3
Printed in Hong Kong

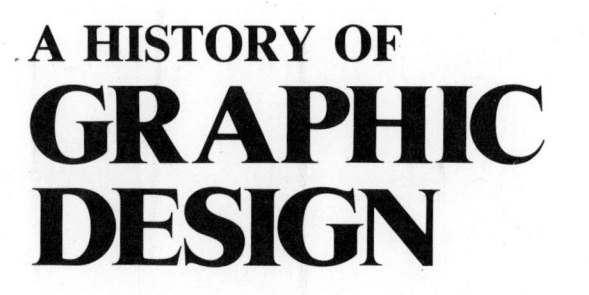

A HISTORY OF
GRAPHIC
DESIGN